THE NEVER ENDING GIFTS

A Starter Kit for New Christians

by
Kris Lindsey

INSPIRE PRESS
Sacramento, CA

THE NEVER ENDING GIFTS
A Starter Kit for New Christians

ISBN_978-1-938196-11-9
Library of Congress Control Number: 2017902116

Inspire Press
PO Box 276794
Sacramento, CA 95670
United States of America
http://inspirewriters.com/inspire-press

Cover photo: Cross of grass © Hein Schlebusch 123rf.com image ID: 10715244

Printed in United States of America

TABLE OF CONTENTS

WHAT IS A CHRISTIAN?

A Christian is a person who has entered into a relationship with God through Jesus Christ. We need to go through Jesus because, as God's perfect Son, Jesus was the only one who could bridge the gap between us and God. We've all done things we shouldn't—things that hurt others and ourselves, and these sins separate us from our Holy God. Jesus came to earth to pay the penalty for these sins so we could be reconciled with God.

The Bible says:

For God so loved the world, that he gave his only Son, that whoever believes in him should not perish but have eternal life. (John 3:16, ESV)

If you believe in Jesus, you can accept his payment on the cross for your sins and enter into a relationship with God by:

- Asking Jesus to forgive your sins.
- Inviting Jesus to come into your life and lead you.

Your prayer may sound something like this:

"Dear Jesus, thank you for dying on the cross to pay for my sins. Please forgive me for the wrong and hurtful things I've done, and come into my life and lead me in your ways. Amen."

If you made the decision to invite Jesus into your life, and prayed a prayer like the one above to invite him in, congratulations! You received the greatest gift ever. To find out what that gift includes, just turn the page.

CHAPTER 1

To You, From God

So then, just as you received Christ Jesus as Lord,
continue to live your lives in him. (Colossians 2:6, NIV)

"Dear God, I don't know you very well, but I want to. Please forgive my sins and come into my life." I opened my eyes and took in the view around me—same university buildings I'd seen a minute before, but something was different. In my heart I knew something big had just happened—something wonderful and good. But I wasn't sure what.

My friend Miriam's eyes twinkled above her broad smile. We stood up, brushed the grass from our knees, and strolled to our next class.

Maybe when you invited Jesus into your life, you also sensed something significant happened.

It did.

When you and I prayed that heartfelt prayer, we received the greatest gift ever: Jesus. Whether we sensed it or not, Jesus came in. And in Jesus, we received three more gifts right there and then.

The first gift was forgiveness for all the sins we ever committed. At that moment, they were lifted off our shoulders—completely paid for and forever forgotten. Not only that, we gained forgiveness through Jesus for all our future sins as well. We are now totally covered.

At the same time, we received our second gift—God's Holy Spirit. The moment we invited Jesus into our life, the Holy Spirit entered our heart. When he did, he gave us the gift of new life by bringing *our* spirit to life. We were spiritually born again.

As if that wasn't enough, the Holy Spirit made our spirit alive for all eternity. When we received Jesus, the third gift we received was eternal life with God—not starting when we die, but now. The Bible says:

> And this is the testimony: that God gave us eternal life, and this life is in his Son. Whoever has the Son has life; whoever does not have the Son of God does not have life. I write these things to you who believe in the name of the Son of God that you may know that you *have* eternal life. (1 John 5:11–13, ESV, emphasis added)

Since we now have the Son, Jesus, in our life, this passage assures us we also have—not *will have*, but *have*—eternal life. Now. Present tense. From here forward. Our never ending life with God has begun.

Wow. Eternal life. Spiritual rebirth. Complete forgiveness. A lot *did* happen when we received Jesus.

Now What?

You made the big decision to ask Jesus to be the Lord of your life. You prayed and invited him in. Now you're standing on the other side of that hurdle wondering what you should *do*.

Should you march down to the local soup kitchen and volunteer? Should you buy some conservative clothes and change your hair to look the part? Should you (gulp) become a missionary to some poverty-stricken third world country?

Thankfully, we don't have to wonder what Jesus wants us to do. He said in Revelation 3:20, "Here I am! I stand at the door and knock. If anyone hears my voice and opens the door, I will come in and eat with that person, and they with me" (ESV).

You and I already heard Jesus knocking, opened the door, and let him in. Now, as with any guest, Jesus wants us to spend time getting to know him—to engage in some hearty dinner conversation.

God already knows us, because, well, he is God. He knew us before we were born, and knows every detail of our life including the number of hairs on our head. God is not concerned with the type of clothes we wear or our hairstyle. He is not even impressed with the things we do for him. What matters most to God is our heart.

God loves us unconditionally and completely. What God wants is for us to love him back.

Jesus said the greatest commandment—the most important thing for us to do—is to "love the Lord your God with all your heart and with all your soul and with all your mind and with all your strength" (Mark 12:30, ESV). In order to love someone, we first need to get to know them.

This is our first assignment: get to know Jesus.

To help us with this assignment, God gave us three more gifts.

Three More Gifts

When we opened the door of our heart to Jesus, the first three gifts—forgiveness, the Holy Spirit, and eternal life—appeared like flowers delivered on our doorstep, fragrant and beautiful to behold.

To help us develop our relationship with Jesus, navigate through trials and tribulations, and to help enrich our lives, God gave us three more gifts, covered in paper and ribbon, ready to unwrap. They are:

- The Bible
- Prayer
- Church

You may be thinking *Oh, those. I know what they are. I've tried reading the Bible, but it didn't make sense. And I'm not convinced that prayer works.* The thought of walking into a church with unfamiliar customs and people may cause your hands to sweat. Besides, what would you wear?

How could plain packages like these possibly hold anything great? Would it even be worth the effort to open them and see?

You may say, "What's the big deal? Can't I just take a pass on these gifts and 'do God' by myself?" The truth is, in order to live life with God we need God's help. We need God's resources.

Although these packages may seem dull on the outside, they do indeed contain treasure beyond measure. They hold keys that unlock ancient mysteries. Through them, we can find the meaning of life, our purpose, and direction. They contain precious healing salves that can remove the pain of deep emotional scars and unleash freedom like nothing on this earth can.

Through them, our heart finds acceptance and belonging, along with the priceless pearls of peace and joy.

With these gifts we have everything we need to live an abundant life, because they help us connect to the source of life, hope, and strength—God Almighty himself. This is not to say that a life with Christ is a life without trouble or pain. It means we have God to help bring us victoriously through whatever life brings.

What a waste it would be to leave these treasures sitting on a shelf in their unopened boxes. Just think of the joy and peace we would miss out on, the opportunities for healing and fulfillment we would pass by.

Opening the Gifts

At my family's birthday and Christmas gatherings, we usually exchange gifts. Occasionally the ribbon around a box is tied too tightly, or the packaging tape is too strong. No worries—my brother-in-law, Cliff, always has his pocket knife handy to open the package with ease.

Likewise, the Bible, prayer, and church are sometimes hard for us to get into. We need help to get started. This book is a handy tool that cuts through the obstacles so we can receive the riches God has for us.

Get ready to receive the awesome, fulfilling treasure found in Jesus.

CHAPTER 2

Unwrapping the Church

But to all who did receive him [Jesus], who believed in his name,
he gave the right to become children of God. (John 1:12, ESV)

Welcome to God's family! When you and I believed in and received Jesus, God gave us the gift of son-ship or daughter-ship. We are now God's children. And as incredible as it may sound, Jesus is now our brother—we have the same Heavenly Father. In fact, everyone who has received Jesus is our brother or sister. All Christians are members of one big family.

This family includes people in our community, our country, and all around the world. Together, we call our family "the church." The church is not a building, or a set of rituals or customs. The church is people. The church is "us."

In each city, members of our church family gather together in smaller groups called "local churches." These churches come in all sizes and have many names. Some are formal, some are casual. Some worship in quiet order, some with emotional release. Church personalities are as varied as the people in them. There are churches to fit everyone.

Though worship styles may differ, these churches have two basic beliefs in common: they all believe in the same God—Father, Son, and Holy Spirit—known as "The Trinity," and they all believe that we can know Jesus personally.

Common Misconceptions

Many images come to mind when people hear the word "church." Some think of church as a stuffy place filled with snooty people. Some think Christians in the church are supposed to be perfect. People who think this way may either feel like they wouldn't fit in, or feel outraged when a Christian's behavior doesn't meet their high expectations.

The truth is, Christians are just people like you and me. We all bring different stories and baggage to church. Each of us begins our Christian journey at a different place, and none of us has arrived at perfection. As C.S. Lewis explained in *Mere Christianity*, Christians are not nicer than other people; they're just nicer than they were before they became Christians.

We Christians are ordinary people seeking an extraordinary God. We come to church with a desire to worship God, to do what's right, and to learn to love more. We are all in various stages of becoming more loving like Christ, with God's help. Church is a place to learn and grow together.

A Lesson from the Barbecue Pit

In the summertime, my husband loves to barbecue on his old reliable charcoal grill. After years of practice, he knows the bigger the coal heap, the easier the fire starts. A lone briquette has a hard time maintaining its heat, but together their shared warmth builds until they all glow.

In the same way, God knows it's difficult to grow in our faith by ourselves, so he gave us a community of people to help us.

On Sunday mornings, the church worship team helps us open our hearts to God through song. The Pastor's sermons give us a deeper understanding of God's message to us in the Bible. As we sit shoulder to shoulder with our church family—united in the purpose of worshiping and learning about God—our spirits lift. Together, we encourage one another.

Our church family experience continues beyond Sunday mornings. During the week, small groups meet to study the Bible or get to know one another through fun activities. This is where I've received answers to my Bible questions, help in applying God's principles to my everyday life, and prayer for myself and my family. People I didn't even know until I joined the group quickly became as close as a sister or brother because of our common bond of seeking and experiencing life with Jesus.

Our Motive Matters

Although many blessings await us at church, if we go just for what we can get out of it, we may be disappointed. The worship leader may choose some songs we don't like, or even sing off key. If people don't smile at us, we might feel unwelcome.

But if we go to give of ourselves, we'll get the full benefit from church. When we give to God by singing the words of the songs as prayers to him, our open hearts connect with him in an intimate way and we feel God's love and power. Any stray notes we may hear won't matter a bit.

When we go to give, we look for the person who's sitting alone, sit next to them, and give them our smile. Chances are, we'll get it right back.

A Gift to Give

To help us encourage one another and build up the church, God gives every Christian a "spiritual gift." A spiritual gift is a new ability or talent we didn't have before.

For example, you may now have the gift of: service, teaching, encouraging, hospitality, giving, leadership, mercy, discernment, craftsmanship, or administration. A great way to discover your particular gift is by volunteering at church. Ask God to show you a place where you could help. Listen to feedback from church leaders and others to help identify your new area of ability.

Sometimes people try out several roles before they find their area of gifting. In the meantime, volunteering helps us get to know people and feel more a part of our church family. When we do discover our spiritual gift, we experience the joy and fulfillment of helping others with the power given by the Holy Spirit.

Church Helps Us Get to Know God

In church, we learn about God in ways we couldn't on our own. The pastor and others who have studied the Bible pass on the truths they've learned to us. This gives us a head start in understanding what the Bible says about God.

When we talk with people in our church family, we see how God is working in their lives. This encourages us to get to know God by including him in our everyday lives, too.

God is love. One way we get to know him is by loving one another. Jesus said, "Whatever you did for one of the least of these brothers and sisters of mine, you did for me" (Matthew 25:40, NIV). When we practice loving our brothers and sisters at church, we practice loving Jesus.

Get Started: Find a Church

Two signs of a good church:

- Belief in the Trinity—three persons in one God: Father, Son, and Holy Spirit.
- Belief in a personal relationship with Jesus as Lord of our lives.

If you already attend a church that holds these beliefs—great. If not, pray and ask God to help you find one. Maybe God will bring to mind a Christian friend who could recommend a good church. Ask for God's guidance as you search church websites for clues about their beliefs, culture, and size.

Select a few churches you think God may be leading you to, and then go visit them two or three times. When you find one with sound beliefs and a personality that fits you, get ready to settle in and get to know your new church family.

Jump In: Encourage Somebody

On your way to church, pray and ask God to help you encourage someone there. Then look for the opportunity God provides. It may be as simple as opening the door for someone, picking up a Sunday school paper a child dropped, or saying a kind word. Church is a place where Christians encourage one another. God loves to help us do this.

CHAPTER 3

Unwrapping the Bible

All Scripture is inspired by God and is useful
to teach us what is true. (2 Timothy 3:16, NLT)

The Bible is the most amazing book in the history of the world. It was written by 40 people over a period of 1550 years, yet has a consistent theme and story. What other book can make that claim? The Bible is a true treasure, with pearls of wisdom from King Solomon, historical insights on ancient civilizations such as Babylon, epic stories of peasants and kings, and much more. It reveals the mystery of how to connect with the God of the universe, and the way to find fulfillment and peace.

With an estimated 100 million copies sold or distributed annually, the Bible is considered to be the most widely circulated book of all time. Chances are a Bible has been on a shelf in your home or in the drawer of a hotel room you slept in. Maybe you even dusted it off and tried reading a few pages. Perhaps you read the whole thing.

If you tried reading the Bible in the past and had a hard time understanding it, don't feel discouraged. That's not unusual. But now when you read it things will be different, because you're different.

The Bible is a spiritual book, inspired by God, and can only be fully discerned with the aid of the Holy Spirit. Since you now have the Holy Spirit living inside you, he will help you understand what you're reading.

Bible Overview

If you are not familiar with the Bible, its unique format and style may seem overwhelming and confusing. Below is a quick overview to get you started.

The Bible is a collection of books, divided into two sections: the Old Testament and the New Testament. The first three-quarters of the Bible is the Old Testament, and the final quarter is the New Testament.

The Old Testament begins with the story of God creating the world. God places his final creations, Adam and Eve, in a lush garden where he gives them tasks and talks with them. But when Eve and Adam break God's only commandment by eating the fruit from the tree of the knowledge of good and evil, he must banish them from the garden. Their sin now separates them from fellowship with God.

For the rest of the Old Testament, God prepares the way to restore his relationship with humankind so we can have fellowship with him again. Through Abraham, God forms a nation—Israel—from which our Savior, the Messiah, will come. Through Moses, he gives them a religious system of laws and sacrifices to teach them who God is, to help them function as a society, and to enable them to recognize the Messiah when he comes.

The New Testament begins with the arrival of the promised Messiah or "Christ" Jesus, God's own Son. Through four accounts of Jesus' life—the books of Matthew, Mark, Luke, and John—we gain insight into who Jesus really is, as we read about the miracles he performs, the lessons he teaches, his death on the cross, and his resurrection. Here we see Jesus' sacrifice that opens the way to our fellowship with God again.

After this, the book of Acts picks up Jesus' story just before he ascends back to heaven. It then goes on to tell how the early Christian church starts, and how the good news of Jesus spreads to the world.

A series of letters comes next, named after their recipients or authors. For example, the book of Romans is a letter written to the church in Rome. These letters explain what Christianity is about, give guidelines for the church, and show how Jesus transforms believers' lives.

In the last book of the Bible—the book of Revelation—the disciple John writes the visions God gave him of the future. Through dream-like symbolism, John describes the terrible series of events leading up to Jesus' second coming, and the final uniting of heaven and earth.

The Bible contains such a wealth of information, a person could spend their whole life studying all the historical facts, lessons taught, and prophesies fulfilled. Although the Bible contains enough answers to satisfy the most curious scholar, at its heart is a simple message a child can understand.

The Ultimate Help Menu and More

I love all the new electronic devices available today, but technology is getting so complex and moving so fast it's hard to keep up. I know, however, whenever I'm at a loss to operate the latest model or update, I can always go to the help menu. There I'll find instructions on how to work my new toy.

We humans are also complex, and live in a rapidly changing society. Sometimes we have deep questions like, "Who am I?" and "What's my purpose?" At other times we get so overwhelmed all we want to know is, "How can I get through this day?" Wouldn't it be nice if we had a help menu to answer our questions and help us thrive? Guess what—we do!

God, our Maker, who knows our unique characteristics, gave us a help menu—the Bible—that tells how we can live with purpose and peace. In it and through it we can learn everything we need to live an abundant life.

But the Bible is more than just a series of instructions for bountiful living. It is a voice from heaven calling, "Please come near. I love you and long to be with you. I love you so much that I gave my only Son so we could be reunited." The Bible is a love letter to you and me from our Heavenly Father.

More than that, the Bible is called the Living Word because as we read it, God speaks directly to our hearts about issues in our lives today. The Bible is a line of communication between God and us.

Digging In

The Bible holds a gold mine of riches. To find the nuggets, though, we have to dig in and read.

Before we can do that, we need to get a Bible with words we can understand. The old standard King James Bible may sound poetic, but its old English is almost as hard to read as Shakespeare. Modern-language Bibles are not only easier to read, many are translated from the oldest Hebrew and Greek manuscripts to ensure accuracy.

Since those who start reading the Bible from the beginning usually get bogged down before they get to the good news about Jesus, the book of Luke in the New Testament is a better place to start. Luke collected eyewitness accounts and compiled the most comprehensive story of Jesus' life. Then Luke continued this story of the early church in the book of Acts. Together, the books of Luke and Acts give a great overview of the beginnings of Christianity.

The Bible is an interactive book. Each time you read it, remember to pray and ask the Holy Spirit for understanding. Then underline the words and phrases that make an impression on your mind and heart.

The Bible Helps Us Get to Know God

One of the best ways to get to know God is by reading the Bible. Through Old Testament stories, we learn of God's power, his patience, and his faithfulness to his people. In the New Testament we see God himself in Jesus and learn the extent of his love for us.

As we read, God also speaks to us personally about the issues we're dealing with. When words and phrases stand out and we suddenly see how they apply to us right where we are, we know Jesus is with us. We see his wisdom and feel how much he cares.

Get Started: Find a Bible

Find or purchase a modern translation of the Bible. Many Christians like the English Standard Version (ESV) for studying, and the New Living Translation (NLT) for easy reading. If you would like a Bible in paper form, I suggest going to a book store to see the size and legibility of the words before you purchase it. Ask if they have highlighter pens that don't bleed through to the other side of the page. If you want a digital Bible, find one with a *highlighting* feature so you can mark the words and passages you want to remember.

Jump In: Read Your Bible

Do you have two minutes a day to read your Bible? Plan a time when you can spend a few minutes with God each day—perhaps in the morning before you start your day, at a break, or right before you go to bed. Put your Bible within arm's reach of where you will sit. Then commit to read your Bible a minimum of two minutes a day.

Before you start to read, pray and ask the Holy Spirit to help you understand what you're reading. As you read, underline (yes, it's okay) or highlight the words or phrases that stand out to you. Then fill out the Bible Reading Journal at the back of this book.

The sentences, or verses, in the Bible are numbered for easy reference. To cite the verse that stood out to you, write the book of the Bible you found it in, the chapter number (followed by a colon), and the number of the verse. For example, Luke 2:11 is the Book of Luke, chapter 2, verse 11.

Bible Reading Journal Example

Date: *Jan. 12*   Verse(s) that stood out: *Luke 2:10–11*
What it said: *"Do not be afraid...I bring you good news...today a Savior has been born"*
What it said to me: *I don't need to be afraid. Jesus is here to save me—good news!*

CHAPTER 4

Unwrapping Prayer

Ask, and it will be given to you; seek, and you will find; knock,
and it will be opened to you. (Matthew 7:7, ESV)

Imagine someone handing you a phone and saying, "Here's your hotline to heaven. You can call God anytime and ask him any question, discuss any topic, and make any request." Think of the possibilities. What would you ask? What would you say?

Well, we Christians have something even better than a phone number for God. We have prayer. When we pray, we don't need mobile networks that can drop calls or phones that can break. We just talk or think to start our conversation.

And God isn't in some distant location waiting for our call. God is right here with us. His Spirit is in us. We can talk with him wherever we are. We can pray in our home, or while we're traveling from place to place. We can talk with him at work, or at play.

Prayer is simply talking with God. We tell God what's on our hearts and then listen for his response. Prayer is a conversation with our friend Jesus. It's a great way to get to know God.

Our goal is to have conversations with God throughout our day. It's also a good practice to set aside a daily one-on-one time with God, even if it's only for a few minutes.

Here are six suggestions for prayer to help you get started.

Drawing Near to God

God is always with us, but sometimes it doesn't feel like he is. How can we get through the imaginary wall that seems to hide him from us? The Bible says, "Enter his gates with *thanksgiving* and his courts with *praise!*" (Psalm 100:4a, ESV, emphasis added).

Suggestion #1: Give Thanks

Thanking God breaks through our thoughts about ourselves and shifts our focus to God. It's so easy to focus on our problems or the things we don't have. When we stop and thank God for the things we *do* have, this reminds us God can supply our needs and help us with our problems. Thanking God for all he's given us opens our hearts to him.

Suggestion #2: Praise God

Praising God helps us grab onto the reality that Almighty God is here with us. We praise God by remembering who he is and what he has done. When we remember God created billions of stars and planets, including our intricate world, we realize nothing is too difficult for him. When we acknowledge that God knows everything in the past, present, and future, it's easier to trust him to know what's best for our lives. When we remember God is love, the truth sinks in that he loves and adores us completely, just as we are. Praising God reminds us our Mighty God can and will work everything for our good, and this helps us feel closer to him.

Suggestion #3: Confess

There *is* one thing that negatively affects our communication with God. Although our sins were forgiven through Jesus, when we do something wrong, hurt someone, or say something that isn't true, it puts a barrier between us and our holy God. To remove this wall, though, all we need to do is agree with God that what we did was wrong, ask God to forgive us, and ask him to help us do the right thing.

Confess and turn to God. That's it. God instantly forgives us and our relationship is back to good.

Talking with God

Suggestion #4: Discuss

God wants us to tell him about the issues on our hearts. No subject is off limits—we can talk to God about anything. We can tell him how our relationships are going, talk about situations at work, or lay out our financial troubles. We can express all our concerns, our hopes, and our fears. We can tell him how we feel, even if we're angry. He already knows everything about us, but he loves to hear it from us anyway. He loves it when we talk with him. He loves it when we pray.

Suggestion #5: Ask

God invites us to come to him with our requests for ourselves and for others. The Bible says, "Ask, and you will receive, that your joy may be full" (John 16:24b, ESV). God wants to guide us, supply our needs, and give us the desires of our hearts. He just wants us to ask, and no request is too large or too small. God is big enough to answer millions of prayers at a time, so we don't have to worry about bothering him. God loves to help.

The only qualification for requests is that we ask for things he would want us to have. The Bible says, "And we are confident that he hears us *whenever we ask for anything that pleases him*" (1 John 5:14, NLT, emphasis added). God has great plans for us, and like a good parent, he only gives us what's best for us.

Hearing God's Voice

Suggestion #6: Listen

We talk to God the same way we talk to people, but listening to God is different. God rarely speaks with a voice we can hear. He usually communicates by forming an impression in our mind or heart—a nudge pushing us toward what seems to be the right choice. You may say, "How do I know if it's God's voice, or my own?" Since it's sometimes hard to tell, it's good to listen for God's voice from several sources for confirmation before making a decision.

One of the best ways to hear God is through our Bible reading. After asking God for guidance, we can look back at our Bible underlining and notes to see what God has been saying to us recently. We can also read our Bible again and watch for words or phrases that pop out to us. This may be God's way of answering.

Often God speaks to us through other Christians. When we talk to people at church or to other Christian friends, we can listen for words and themes that apply to what we're going through. Frequently, God will bring us together with people who've had similar experiences, and will encourage us with what Jesus is saying and doing in their lives, too.

God sometimes answers us by working to change our circumstances. After we make requests, we can watch to see what happens in the days and weeks to come. God may answer our prayers in a different way than we expected, but it will always be for our good.

One thing is for sure, God's guidance will never contradict the Bible. This is one great reason to read our Bibles and become familiar with what it says. God's advice never causes harm. God always speaks life and goodness. The more we get to know God, the easier it will be to recognize his voice.

The Six Suggestions for Prayer

The suggestions for prayer, as described above, are:

- Give Thanks
- Praise God
- Confess
- Discuss
- Ask
- Listen

Does God Always Answer Our Prayers?

I've heard some people say they prayed, and God didn't answer. But God always answers our prayers—he says yes, no, or wait.

Sometimes God's "yes" is not the answer we expected. Frequently, God has something even better for us than what we requested. When we ask, it's best to be open and look for whatever answer God gives.

When we pray and don't see anything happening, God could be saying "no." Maybe what we thought we wanted wasn't good for us after all.

Sometimes silence is God's way of saying "wait." He wants to give us what we asked for, but the timing isn't right. For example, we may pray for a certain job opportunity, but God knows an even better job will be available soon. If we wait, we can have God's best.

Prayer Helps Us Get to Know God

Prayer is powerful, but its power is not in the prayers themselves. Prayer is only as powerful as the one we're praying to. If we pray to a rock, it cannot answer back. Our prayers are effective because Almighty God is willing and able to answer.

God loves to answer prayers for several reasons. One reason is so we can see he's really here. We ask God for help, and he responds. We toss a ball out into empty space, and someone throws it back. The more we interact with God, the more we'll see how he is actively working in our world. Each time he responds, our trust in him will grow.

God also answers prayers to show us how much he loves us. When we see the loving way God answers our prayers and the prayers of those around us, it touches our hearts and makes us want to love him back.

Ask God questions and make requests throughout the day, then listen and see how he answers. God stands ready to shower us with a never ending supply of gifts, more precious than we can imagine. He's just waiting for us to turn and talk to him. He's waiting for us to ask.

Get Started: Set Up a Prayer Journal

Find a notebook and write "Date" and "Request" on the left side of the page, and "Date" and "God's Answer" on the right.

Date	Request	Date	God's Answer

Jump In: Start Writing Your Requests

After making requests to God, write them in your notebook or on the Prayer Journal page at the back of this book, and then write God's answers to your prayers when you receive them.

CHAPTER 5

New Power

And don't let us yield to temptation, but rescue us
from the evil one. (Matthew 6:13, NLT)

If you could have any super-power, which one would you choose? Maybe the ability to fly or to become invisible? Well, you *do* have a super-power. When you received Jesus you were transformed into a new person—a new creation. Your heart was cleansed, your spirit was reborn, and the Holy Spirit now living inside you gives you the super-power to resist temptation.

Resisting temptation may not sound like a super-power until we think about it. How many times do we succumb to the same old habits and vices? We try to muster the strength to resist, but end up giving in time after time. Maybe it does take a super-power to overcome.

The Temptation Cycle

How does temptation work? Nothing can tempt us unless we already have the desire for it. If I don't like chocolate, then even the richest chocolaty hot-fudge-drizzled dessert can't tempt me. The Bible says:

> Temptation comes from our own desires, which entice us and drag us away. These desires give birth to sinful actions. And when sin is allowed to grow, it gives birth to death. (James 1:14-15, NLT)

God can help us change these desires over time, but in the meantime, the super power from God's Holy Spirit can help us stop this sin cycle before our desires turn into actions.

Overcoming Temptation

The first inkling that we have this new power to overcome will most likely come when we start to do something we shouldn't. It may not have bothered us much to do it before, but now we're painfully aware that it is wrong. This pang, which feels like a super-conscience, is the Holy Spirit's way of convicting us, his way of urging us to stop.

God knows we are all tempted to do things that are bad for us and for others, so along with the Holy Spirit's warning signal, he provides an additional way for us to resist. The Bible says:

> The temptations in your life are no different from what others experience. And God is faithful. He will not allow the temptation to be more than you can stand. When you are tempted, he will show you a way out so that you can endure. (1 Corinthians 10:13, NLT)

When we are tempted, God will provide a "way out" by giving us another option that is the right thing to do. Our job is to stop and look for that option, to ask the Holy Spirit for strength to take it, and then to trust God for the results. This may feel a bit like a trapeze move—we may need to let go of the familiar bad option before we can grab hold of the new good one, and the space in between may seem scary. But as we see how God comes through and how the good choices turn out, our confidence to trust God will grow.

It's Not Just Us

It helps me to know that when I'm tempted, it's not just me. We have a spiritual enemy, the devil, who looks for our weaknesses and fears, and then places temptations in our path. This father of all lies wants to trip us up so we'll become discouraged and think *I'm not really a Christian. I'm not good enough.* Don't believe these thoughts. They don't come from God, and they are not true. When we received Jesus, we became Christians based on what *Jesus* did, not on our own merit. Because Jesus paid the price for every bad thing we've ever done, we are clean and righteous. We are new creations, God's precious children—fully loved and accepted just as we are. And we are all in various stages of becoming more like Jesus. None of us is perfect.

The Bible says, "Resist the devil, and he will flee from you" (James 4:7b, ESV). When we face temptation, we can foil the enemy's plot by saying, "No, I'm not stepping into this trap. God, please fill me with your Holy Spirit's power and show me a better way." When the devil sees we're not falling for his old tricks—that we're trusting God and he's going to lose—he will go away. And the power boost from the Holy Spirit will give us the strength to make a better choice.

Sometimes the enemy's tactics are subtle. He may throw all kinds of distractions in our way—bad or good—to sidetrack us from following Jesus. If certain activities, lifestyle patterns, or friends keep you from going to church, hanging out with Christians, or spending time praying and reading your Bible, this could be the devil's way of putting a damper on God's power in your life. Take time to assess the obstacles in your way, and then ask God to help you remove them. If certain places or friends entice you into old bad habits, then it might be wise to stay away from them for a while.

We need to be aware of the enemy's methods, but not concerned. His power is as small as an ant's compared to God's. The devil has no power over us, except what we give him. Once we recognize what he's doing, we can take action and dismiss him.

When We Mess Up

Although we have the power to resist temptation, we all mess up and do the wrong thing sometimes. God knows we have this problem and has provided a solution. The Bible says:

> If we confess our sins, he [God] is faithful and just and will forgive us our sins and purify us from all unrighteousness. (1 John 1:9, NIV)

This Bible promise has two parts: our part and God's part. Our part is to admit that what we did was wrong and tell God we're sorry. Because God is faithful and just, he will do his part and forgive us. More than that, he will also "purify" us.

What does *purify* mean? When water is purified, every speck of dirt is removed until all that's left is 100% pure, sparkling water. When God purifies us, every remnant of wrongdoing is removed and we are totally righteous, clean, and free. We can hold our head high and move forward. We may still need to make restitution with other people, but our burden of guilt is gone.

Our Never Ending Power Source

God has given us everything we need to overcome temptation. Jesus took away our sins and gave us a fresh start as new, spiritually reborn creations. Now when we face temptation, we have the Holy Spirit's warning signal and power to stop. We also have access to God's wisdom to guide us away from trouble. God even provided a way to restore us when we mess up.

As we learn more and more about who God is and how unconditionally he loves us, the hurts we're trying to soothe in unhealthy ways will heal. Then the temptations of our old life won't be so appealing. God will replace our old desires with new ones that bring life and fulfillment—the abundant life God intends for us to have.

Turning to God when we face temptation also builds our relationship with him. God knows about the things we struggle with. When we let down our defenses and ask him to help, this frees him to pour out endless supplies of provision, power, and peace on us. With God's help, we can live victoriously.

Get Started: Memorize 1 Corinthians 10:13b

Copy the verse below on a card and put it somewhere you will see it every day, like on your refrigerator door or bathroom mirror. Memorizing Bible verses helps us impress God's truths on our minds and makes it easier to recognize and dismiss the enemy's lies.

God is faithful. He will not allow the temptation to be more than you can stand. When you are tempted, he will show you a way out so that you can endure. (1 Corinthians 10:13b, NLT)

Jump In: Practice

Practice saying this verse word-for-word every day for a week, and then twice a week for a month to pack it away in your long term memory. Repeat the verse twice a month after that to keep it fresh in your mind.

After you recite the verse, mark the date below.

Day 1 ❏   Day 2 ❏   Day 3 ❏
Day 4 ❏   Day 5 ❏   Day 6 ❏
Day 7 ❏

Week 2 ❏ ❏   Week 3 ❏ ❏   Week 4 ❏ ❏
Week 5 ❏ ❏

Month 2 ❏ ❏   Month 3 ❏ ❏   Month 4 ❏ ❏
Month 5 ❏ ❏   Month 6 ❏ ❏

CHAPTER 6

Pass It On

For what I received I passed on to you... (1 Corinthians 15:3a, NIV)

Here we sit, with scraps of crumpled wrapping paper scattered around. We survey our gifts and see the bouquet of Forgiveness, Spiritual Rebirth, and Eternal Life that arrived on our doorstep in Chapter 1. Next to these, we see our "Child of God" name badges and our Spiritual Gifts to help the church from Chapter 2. We pick up our new Bibles and breathe in the leather scent. The shiny gold page edges hint at the treasures stored inside. Then our gaze lands on the journals labeled "Answered Prayers," just waiting to be filled. Draped over a chair-back, we see our red capes with the words "Power to Overcome."

Wow, what a haul. And these gifts are just the start. An endless supply of blessings awaits us as our relationship with Jesus grows deeper.

These free gifts are so wonderful, so empowering, and so life-changing that we can't just keep them to ourselves. We'll want to tell everyone about Jesus so they can have these gifts, too.

Spread the Joy

We can start by telling the Christians we know the news that we invited Jesus into our lives. Did someone in your past talk to you about accepting Jesus as Lord and Savior? Who do you think may have been praying for you? Give them a call and tell them you asked Jesus to come in and lead your life. Spread the joy and practice sharing your good news with them.

At church, tell your pastor or small group leader about your decision to receive Christ. It'll make their day, and they may be able to suggest resources to help you grow in your faith.

The Best Gift to Give

What's the best gift you've ever given someone? Well, you now have an even greater gift to offer—Jesus. He can help people wherever they are, whenever they need it, and his gifts will last for eternity. Sounds good, but you may be thinking *I don't know how to tell someone about Jesus.*

You'll be happy to know that you won't need to stand on a street corner and shout about Jesus as people rush by. You don't even need more Bible knowledge. The best way to spread the news about Jesus is to tell the people around you the story of how you came to have Jesus in your life.

Everyone enjoys a good story. A story gets a point across in a friendly, non-threatening way. You're an expert on the subject of how you came to Jesus because you lived it. People will be interested in hearing about something that made an impact on your life.

It's a good idea to think about our story ahead of time so we can tell it without rambling. Below is a model for a short version of our story in three parts: the *before*, the *how*, and the *after*.

The Before

In the "before," we talk about what motivated us to move toward God. For many people, this was some sort of problem or crisis. Since these kinds of situations are sometimes difficult to talk about, and since not all people had similar experiences and will be able to relate, it's usually better to talk about how we *felt* rather than explaining all the details.

Feelings are universal. If I said, "I felt so ashamed," my statement would relate as well to a child who stole a treat from a cookie jar as it would to an adult with a shady past. Everyone can relate to feelings. The circumstances that produced these feelings vary, but the feelings are the same.

In your *before,* you'll want to describe the feelings that motivated you to seek Jesus, and what you did as a result. In my story, I say, "I felt like my world was out of control, so I set out to see if God was real and active here on earth."

The How

In the "how," we spell out the specifics of when it was, where we were, who we were with, and what we said when we asked Jesus into our life. If you did this recently, this part will be easy to put together. If it has been awhile, pray and ask the Holy Spirit to help you remember.

Take a minute and picture the place where you asked Jesus into your life. Were you outside or indoors? If you were indoors, what room were you in? If you were in a church, were you near the back or the front? The more specific the descriptions, the more real the event will be to your listener.

Were you with someone when you received Jesus? If so, include their name. If you were alone, say you were by yourself.

When did this take place? Do you know the exact date? If not, do you remember the month or season or year?

For the last part of the *how,* try to say the words or meaning of what you said when you invited Jesus into your life. If you don't remember, ask the Holy Spirit to help bring your prayer back to mind. If you were with someone, you might ask them if they remember what you said. Be sure to include the parts about asking Jesus to forgive your sins, and inviting him to be the Lord of your life.

Say your prayer as if you are saying it now. For example, you might say, "Then I said, 'Dear Jesus, please forgive my sins, come into my heart, and lead my life.'" When the person hears the words you prayed, they will know how they can ask Jesus into their life.

The After

In the "after" we talk about the changes we noticed right after we prayed. Think back to the moment after your prayer, to the scene around you, and what you felt. What new awareness did you have about yourself and God? How did you feel about God in the hours and days that followed?

For me, I knew my sins were forgiven. I knew for sure that God was real. And I was aware that I had a powerful friend in Jesus who would always be there for me.

Passing the Gift On

After putting together your story, or "testimony," ask God for the opportunity to tell it to someone who doesn't know Jesus. Then watch to see who God brings around.

When the opportunity arises, tell the person your prepared story, and then ask if they have ever prayed a prayer like you did. If they have, then you can enjoy listening to their story.

If they have never invited Jesus into their life, ask them if they'd like to. If they say "yes," let them know that the Bible says God loves us so much that he sent his son, Jesus, to pay for our sins by dying on a cross:

> For God so loved the world, that he gave his only Son, that whoever believes in him should not perish but have eternal life. (John 3:16, ESV)

If they believe that God's Son, Jesus, died for their sins, and they want to receive his forgiveness and follow him, explain how they can invite Jesus in by saying their own two-part prayer like this:

- Ask Jesus to forgive your sins.
- Invite Jesus to come into your life and lead you. Amen.

After they pray, smile at your new brother or sister and say, "Welcome to God's family." Then help them unwrap their gifts from God so they can enjoy them, too.

Get Started: Write Your Testimony

Using the instructions from the previous pages, fill in the worksheet below to create an outline. The goal is to tell a short version of your story in one to three minutes. Once you get the basic facts down, you may want to write a short introduction and add a few details to make the story flow.

Jump In: Tell Your Story

Practice saying your story out loud until the words come naturally. Ask God to provide the opportunity for you to tell it to someone, then when he does, take a deep breath and let them know how you invited Jesus into your life.

My Testimony Worksheet

My Before:

I felt _____,

so I (explain what you did that led you to God) _____

_____

_____

_____

My How:

When: _____

Where: _____

With whom: _____

What I prayed: I said, "_____

_____

_____

_____."

My After:

Then I knew/was aware that (write what was different) _____

_____

_____

_____

_____

_____

BIBLE STUDY

God

Father, Son, and Holy Spirit

God is described as "the Trinity," one God in three persons—Father, Son, and Holy Spirit. To help you get to know our wonderful God, we'll look closely at a few Bible verses that describe who God is and some things he does. If possible, ask a Christian friend or a mentor at church to study these verses with you.

Before you begin the study, pray and ask the Holy Spirit to help you understand the Bible verses. Then read the Bible verses and answer the questions by looking back to the verses to find the answer.

God the Father

Bible verse:

For God so loved the world, that he gave his only Son, that whoever believes in him should not perish but have eternal life. (John 3:16, ESV)

1. According to this verse, who does God love?

2. Who does "the world" include?

3. Does "the world" include you?

4. Then who does God love?

5. Looking back at the verse, what did God the Father do to show how much he loves you?

Bible verse:

God has said, "Never will I leave you; never will I forsake you." (Hebrews 13:5b, NIV)

6. In this verse, what two things does God say he will never do?

7. What does it mean to "leave" someone?

8. How long is *never*?

9. So, how long will God stay with you?

10. Write two things you learned about God the Father from John 3:16 and Hebrews 13:5b.

God the Son

Bible verses:

[30]"Don't be afraid, Mary," the angel told her, "for you have found favor with God! [31]You will conceive and give birth to a son, and you will call him Jesus"... [34]Mary asked the angel, "But how can this happen? I am a virgin." [35]The angel replied, "The Holy Spirit will come upon you, and the power of the Most High will overshadow you. So the baby to be born will be holy, and he will be called the Son of God." (Luke 1:30–31, 34–35, NLT)

1. According to verse 35, how was Jesus conceived?

2. Who was Jesus' mother?

3. According to verse 35, who is Jesus' father?

4. Since Jesus inherited his "human nature" from his mother, Mary, and his "God nature" from his father, God, Jesus was both fully God and fully _____.

5. Since God the Son is also human, how does this help you relate to him?

Bible verses:

¹In the beginning the Word already existed. The Word was with God, and the Word was God. ²He existed in the beginning with God. ³God created everything through him, and nothing was created except through him...¹⁴So the Word became human and made his home among us...And we have seen his glory, the glory of the Father's one and only Son. (John 1:1–3, 14, NLT)

6. We know Jesus is the "Word" because verse 14 (the last verse above) says the Word became human, lived among us, and is God's one and only Son. Read the verses again substituting "Jesus" for "the Word," "He," and "him."

7. The very end of verse 1 says Jesus (the Word) was _____. God the Son is the second person of the Trinity.

8. In verses 1 and 2, who was with God (the Father) in the beginning?

9. Verse 3 says everything was created through Jesus. What do you think "everything" includes?

10. Since Jesus is God, and created everything in the universe, including you and me, would any problem in your life be too difficult for Jesus to help you with?

God the Holy Spirit

Bible verses:

¹³And when you believed in Christ, he identified you as his own by giving you the Holy Spirit, whom he promised long ago. ¹⁴The Spirit is God's guarantee that he will give us the inheritance he promised and that he has purchased us to be his own people. He did this so we would praise and glorify him. (Ephesians 1:13b–14, NLT)

1. According to verse 13, when we believed in Christ Jesus, what did he give us?

2. Again in verse 13, what does a person have to do to be given the Holy Spirit?

3. Verse 14 says the Holy Spirit is God's guarantee that he will give us the _____ he promised (which would include eternal life), and his guarantee that he has purchased us to be his _____.

Bible verse:

Or do you not know that your body is a temple of the Holy Spirit within you, whom you have from God? (1 Corinthians 6:19a, ESV)

4. A temple is a building that God inhabits. In this verse, what are Christian's bodies compared to?

5. According to the verse, where is God's Holy Spirit?

6. If God the Holy Spirit is within us, is God ever far away?

Bible verse:

But the Helper, the Holy Spirit, whom the Father will send in my name, he will teach you all things and will bring to remembrance all that I have said to you. (John 14:26, ESV)

7. According to this verse, what are two things the Holy Spirit does?

8. Since the Holy Spirit will teach us all things, can he help us understand the Bible?

9. Can the Holy Spirit help us remember what God says in the Bible?

10. Looking back on all three Bible passages about God the Holy Spirit:

    Who has the Holy Spirit? (hint: see question 2)

    Where is the Holy Spirit? (hint: see question 5)

    How does the Holy Spirit help us? (hint: see question 7)

The grace of the Lord Jesus Christ and the love of God and the fellowship of the Holy Spirit be with you all. (2 Corinthians 13:14, ESV)

BIBLE READING JOURNAL

Prayer: "Dear God, please speak to my heart and help me understand your Word as I read. In Jesus' name I pray, amen."

Date: _____ Verse(s) that stood out: _____
What it said: _____
_____
What it said to me: _____
_____

Date: _____ Verse(s) that stood out: _____
What it said: _____
_____
What it said to me: _____
_____

Date: _____ Verse(s) that stood out: _____
What it said: _____
_____
What it said to me: _____
_____

Date: _____ Verse(s) that stood out: _____
What it said: _____
_____
What it said to me: _____
_____

Date: _____ Verse(s) that stood out: _____
What it said: _____
_____
What it said to me: _____
_____

Date: _____ Verse(s) that stood out: _____
What it said: _____
_____
What it said to me: _____
_____

Date: _____ Verse(s) that stood out: _____
What it said: _____
_____
What it said to me: _____
_____

PRAYER JOURNAL

Date	Request	Date	God's Answer

CPSIA information can be obtained
at www.ICGtesting.com
Printed in the USA
BVOW10s1105290517
485357BV00004B/5/P